Trail of Hearts
A Decade of Love Poems

A Collection of 10 poems written over 10 years

Tiina Susanna Farin

Balboa Press books may be ordered through booksellers or by contacting:

Balboa Press
A Division of Hay House
1663 Liberty Drive
Bloomington, IN 47403
www.balboapress.com
1 (877) 407-4847

ISBN: 978-1-5043-3092-3 (sc)
ISBN: 978-1-5043-3093-0 (e)

Library of Congress Control Number: 2015905597

Print information available on the last page.

Balboa Press rev. date: 07/08/2015

BALBOA
PRESS
A DIVISION OF HAY HOUSE

This book is dedicated to every single person out there.

Allow me to explain how this book came to be.

I have been writing poems since I was 11 years old but never had the intention of publishing any of them, as they were initially simply a form of release and the expression of my most private thoughts and feelings.

I have also loved the art of photography ever since
I took a high school photography class.

And lastly, there is a special way in which I believe love is speaking to me. In 2009, after spending a weekend in Paris, I was washing dishes and realized my hand was stinging. When I looked at my hand, I giggled out loud as I discovered the source of the sting.

There was a teensy tiny scrape on the top of my hand above the knuckle on my middle finger, no larger than the head of a pin, and it was undeniably in the shape of a heart. Not almost a heart, but a perfectly symmetrical heart. I giggled because it was as though the city of love had literally left its mark on me. Ever since then, I have been blessed to see "hearts" in places one would not expect to see them and began documenting such occurrences. You see, every time one appears for me it is like a gentle nudge or loving smile from the most powerful force on earth. As though love is literally whispering in my ear "remember me." I say they appear for me, because I have always seen them at the most impeccable time. Whatever the reason, be it as a reminder to be more loving in a situation, as the cherry on top of a perfect moment, or simply as a sign along the road that everything is going to be okay, I am just tickled pink each and every time to be kissed by love in this way.

One day, out of pure curiosity I wanted to see if I had enough poems about love to match with the pictures of naturally occurring hearts I had started taking in my 20's.

To my surprise and delight, as I started this process I found that not only did I have exactly 10 poems about love but that I also had the exact, perfect naturally occurring heart picture to pair with it that echoed the tone of the poem. It took no small amount of courage to decide to share this collection publically, as originally this collection too was compiled and intended just for me, as an expression of my self-love.

The poems to follow were written between the years 1996 – 2007, the photos taken between the years 2009-2014, meaning the material in this book spans a period of 18 years. The poems range in emotion from short and sweet to longer, tinged with pain and confusion.

From the high school crush that doesn't even know my
name, to someone I dreamt about years before I met him,
from my first heartbreak, to my heart's deepest desire.

The poems are laid out in chronological order until the very last one.
The last poem jumps back some years, and is one of my deepest wishes
for myself, but also my wish for you all and is shared last so as to leave
those words as my lasting impression on you. I share them with love
from my heart to yours, to tell the tale of loves bitter and sweet stings
in all its many forms, but even more so as a message of inspiration and
encouragement to not give up on love no matter how many times your
heart has been broken. As a single female now in my early 30's, not
yet having experienced true love, I still choose to believe in love. The
knees weak, heart-stopping, catch your breath, fairy-tale kind of love –
not to rescue or complete me, but because I have come to learn it is
my birthright to experience such a happy, loving and healthy union of
souls. All of life comes in pairs. One of the seven laws of the Universe,
the principle of polarity, states that nothing exists without its opposite.
So if I exist, so does my other-half, and if it is out there for me, it is also
out there for you! Know that you are not alone on your journey, but
also know that your love story does not begin when someone falls in
love with you, it begins when you fall in love with yourself. So, while
this book is about the journey to finding true love, it is also about the
lessons learned along the way. The lessons that are meant to grace you
with the lion-heartedness it takes to step out into the world as your
true self so that true love can find you. Know that you are not alone,
but also know that your love story begins with falling in love yourself.

May this book serve as a light that helps illuminate the way,
as you follow your own trail of hearts to find true love!

*"No human relation gives one possession in another—every two
souls are absolutely different. In friendship or in love, the two side
by side raise hands together to find what one cannot reach alone."*

Khalil Gibran

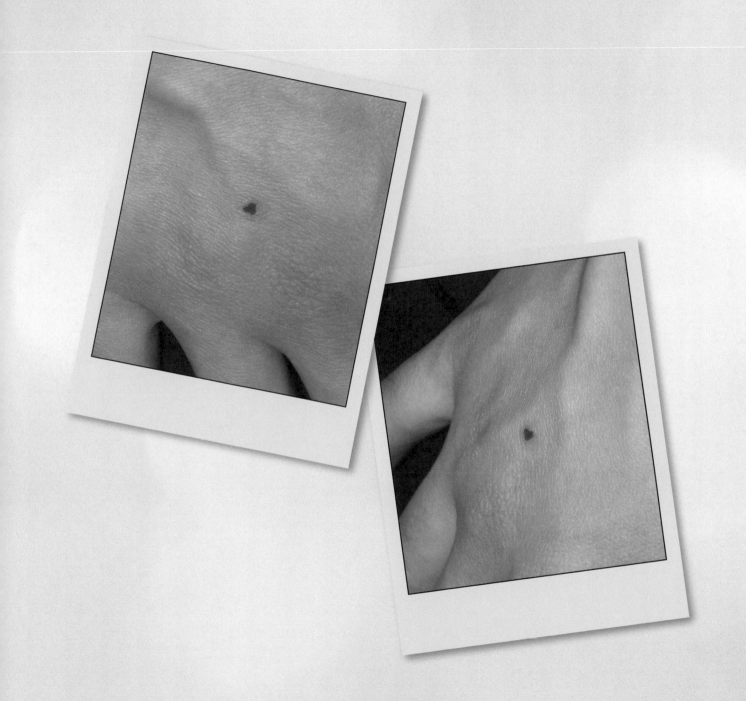

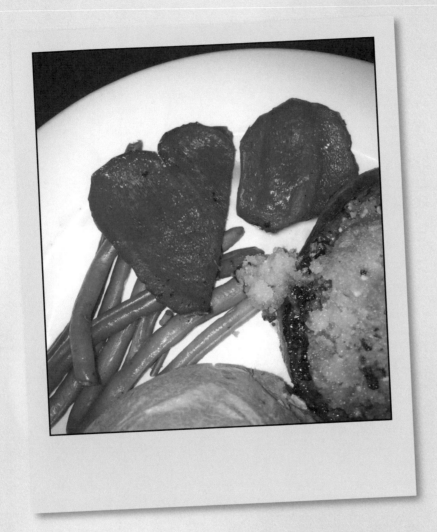

The high school crush that doesn't even know my name…

All of Me

June 27, 1997 – 15 yrs. old

You struck my heart the moment I first laid eyes on you, and
ever since I have wondered if I had struck you too.

You drowned me in those eyes of yours the first time our eyes met. That
face and gorgeous smile of yours, I know I will never forget.

We left each other not knowing if we would ever meet again, and
because of this uncertainty I left with the strangest pain.

There is something I wish you knew, something you should see, which
is, that I am right here and fully willing to give you all of me.

Imagining Love…

Bliss

September 4, 1999 – 17 yrs. old

It's the calm that passes through me, when you whisper in my ear.

It's the conviction you instill in me, whenever you are near.

It's the comfort that your closeness brings, in every breath I take of you.

It's the rush of complete fulfillment, knowing you feel the same way too.

It's all of these things that make our love worth believing in.

And for all of these things I would not doubt surrendering everything.

The boy who just wants to be friends…

Just a friend

September 24, 1999 – 17 yrs. old

The thought of eluding love your whole life really hurts, but thank
goodness it was for you that I was all the while in search.

Now here you are, you know my name, yet distant you still be, for
I could never conceive the thought of you ever loving me.

You make me laugh, I try to smile, yet fearful I remain, because you
flirt and play with everyone and to you I am just a game.

When you're around you could literally see my heartbeat through my skin.
Yet you're also the one that could completely cause it to cave in.

For now I put my dreams aside and hope my heart will mend,
for you and I shall never be and so you stay a friend.

The one who leaves you hanging…

Hanging

September 16, 2000 – 18 yrs. old

Would I be worth a second glance to be the one that you adore?

Would you consider me beautiful enough to want nothing more?

Would I be lucky enough to deserve you if I gave you everything?

Would you be good enough to love me back if I did not stop at anything?

Would I be the one you came to love if together there was nothing we could not do?

Would you be kind enough to let me know? Because I am so in love with you.

Contemplating Love…

Madness

September 23, 2000 – 18 yrs. old

I often wonder if love is just another kind of madness.

A form of insanity wherein our sense of all other things are lulled to sleep.

And in that slumber, all lost causes forgotten and weaknesses
forgive, we desert ourselves into an infallible haven.

Our hearts willfully detained by another human being, we are enraptured.

Comfortably adrift a river of blissful oblivion, guided
by the sheer loveliness of being in love.

It is a strange thing when someone can make you so happy it takes your breath
away, or so happy you could cry. And in those tears your view of all that is
wrong and frightful in the world is glazed over by something glorious.

If love is madness where we are whisked away from
fear and loneliness, it is a beautiful one.

About my first boyfriend…

Untitled

December 8, 2000 – 19 yrs. old

He has a gentle touch. I like the softness of his lips.

He likes the sound of my laughter, and I love the way we kiss.

I like the safety of his arms where he likes to hold me tight.

And I knew we would be together at very first sight.

The Player…

Heart of Stone

October 8, 2001 – 19 yrs. old

It is odd consciousness that seizes me when I am with you. You are like
the wind, in that it is not what I see, but I feel that mystifies me.

I can barely put my finger on what it is about you that enamours me
so. Perhaps it is your charm, or your apprehending presence that
leaves many like myself completely and utterly defenceless.

And when you do not know the potency of your feigned affection, or the spellbinding
illusion it casts, you are like a storm, beautiful but destructive, fickle as the weather itself.

And when the ease of your eventual rejection sets in, you become one in
the same with the person who whomever he touched turned to stone.

Huh…?!?

Conjure

February 10, 2004 – 22 yrs. old

I imagined in you into being from a conjured image in my head. I dreamed up
a face, a name, a body and soul from a distant place beyond my bed.

So imagine my surprise as our paths came to meet, and imagine
my bewilderment as into your eyes I caught a peek.

You felt like home, simple yet true, a feeling I could not explain.

Seeing you before my eyes showed me that dreaming was not in vain.

Yet by my side you could not stay, be it fear of fallacy or both.

Perhaps it was just not the time for us to together coast.

For a moment you were tangible and standing right in front of me, but for
now that moment is in the past, when will I know if we will ever be?

Feeling denied by love…

Untitled

September 14, 2006 – 25 yrs. old

Am I too real? Am I too honest? Am I too vulnerable, or too strong?

Is there no one out there that is the match to whom I could belong?

What is about my character, about my will or my charm, that
is keeping my other half so far away from my arm?

Am I too loving? Am I too sweet? Am I too cherishable to keep?

What is about me that is making my soul-mate so hard to meet?

Am I not ready or deserving to know such kind of love?

What is it? I ask you please, oh divine guidance from above.

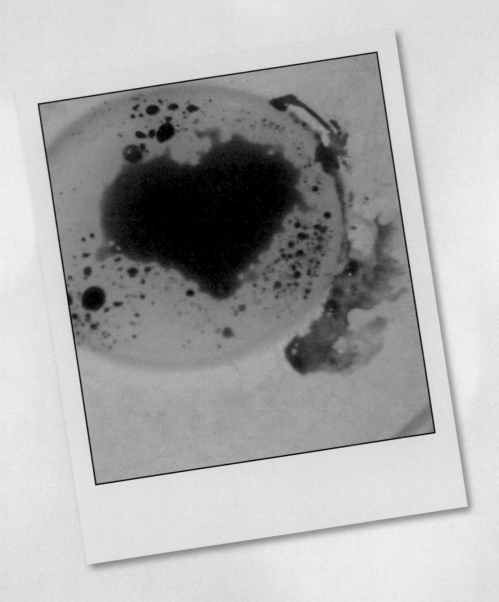

Somewhere

July 29, 2000 – 19 yrs. old

Somewhere out there, and not just in make believe, exists that
special someone with whom I was meant to be.

The person that would be there in the morning as I woke. The
person whose every words I would cling to when he spoke.

The person in whose arms I would feel most at home. The person
that would love me more than I could ever know.

A person that would comfort me when I was weak and small,
the person I knew I would love forever and above all.

A person I swear had fallen straight from Heaven's window sill, full of mercy
and compassion, that even when I was enraged would love me still.

A person that could ease my pain simply with his kiss. The person
with whom I'd know, life could not get much better than this.

The person to whom in instant I would give my heart to take,
and trust that in his hands again it would never break.

A person unlike any other whose eyes I would recognize anywhere,
the person whom I know, is waiting for me somewhere.

Printed in the United States
By Bookmasters